GORGEOUS GEORGIA

Also by Karyn K. Zweifel:

Southern Vampires
Covered Bridge Ghost Stories
Dog-Gone Ghost Stories

GORGEOUS GEORGIA

Compiled by
Karyn K. Zweifel

PREMIUM PRESS AMERICA
Nashville, Tennessee

GORGEOUS GEORGIA by Karyn K. Zweifel

Copyright © 1998 by PREMIUM PRESS AMERICA

All rights reserved. No part of this book may be reproduced or transmitted in any form or by any means, electronic or mechanical, including photocopy, recording, or by any information storage and retrieval system, without the written permission of the Publisher, except where permitted by law.

ISBN 1-887654-36-4

Library of Congress Catalog Card Number 97-76474

PREMIUM PRESS AMERICA books are available at special discounts for premiums, sales promotions, fund-raising, or educational use. For details contact the Publisher at P.O. Box 159015, Nashville, TN 37215-9015, or phone toll free (800) 891-7323 or (615) 256-8484.

Cover by L. Mayhew Gore Art
Layout by Bob Bubnis / BookSetters
Printed by Vaughan Printing

First Edition, June 1998
1 2 3 4 5 6 7 8 9 10

Dedication

To Mary Ann Turner and the whole Hunter and Turner clan—Georgia peaches all—thanks for including me in your family.

Introduction

I was nine before I came to the American South. Once I got here, I decided I never wanted to leave. The lush green landscape, the mild winters, and above all, the people, struck a chord in me. It feels like home here.

I discovered Georgia when I was seventeen and a freshman at LaGrange College, in Western Georgia. Weekends, I would drive all around the countryside, exploring little towns, prowling through old cemeteries and hiking through the woods. The history fascinates me, and the folks I've met have always welcomed me.

Georgia became, for a few short hours, a scary place when my boyfriend took me down its winding rural roads and through its red clay fields to meet his family. It stormed the night we drove over, and I remember the supple cedars lining the road, whipped by the wind, seeming to block our passage with a dark and sinister purpose.

But his mother greeted me with a warm smile. She graciously surrendered her oldest son to a transplanted Midwesterner, and for fifteen years, has treated me to some of the best Southern cooking I've ever tasted. My mother-in-law, her family and friends are the epitome of Georgia to me.

I have gleefully introduced the pleasures of Georgia to my daughter, since it is her true heritage, not an acquired habit like my own. She and I have wandered the narrow country roads and stopped in at the old ramshackle stores to swap stories with folks who treated us like family, even when we weren't. I thank them all for contributing to this book, and to my understanding of the state.

I hope this little book inspires you to look for the Georgia I've found, a place where people always say hello with a smile and invite you to share a meal or a story. It's a great place to visit. Great folks have raised their families there, too, as my husband will tell you and I can confirm.

Many people helped me gather information and verify facts for this project, and I am grateful for their assistance. My office staff, Tabby and Buster, have contributed their best, as has my family. But chiefly I am grateful to God, who has blessed me with a profession that is almost always more fun than work.

Karyn K. Zweifel

 GORGEOUS GEORGIA

1. Georgia entered the Union on January 2, 1788, as the **fourth** state.

2. Here's something to sing about: Brenda Lee, Alan Jackson, Little Richard, Travis Tritt, Ray Stevens, James Brown, Trisha Yearwood, Ray Charles, TLC, Lena Horne, Bill Anderson, the Robert Shaw Chorale, Gladys Knight and the Pips, Ronnie Milsap, Curtis Mayfield, Chet Atkins, Indigo Girls, Ma Rainey, Fletcher Henderson, Harry James, Jessye Norman, Johnny Mercer—all are native Georgians.

3. If you hear that the streets of Atlanta are paved with gold, don't scoff. Building materials from North Georgia frequently have measurable amounts of the metal in them. When the mint in Dahlonega was torn down, the bricks used to build it were crushed and the gold was extracted.

GORGEOUS GEORGIA

4. In the North Georgia mountains, a ranger station is named in honor of Arthur Woody, the "Barefoot Ranger" who created the first wildlife management area in the South. For years, he had the best forest fire protection record in the United States. Even though it was against regulations, Woody refused to wear shoes in the office. He wouldn't listen to his immediate supervisor, so the Regional Forest Supervisor went to Woody's house to make him comply. A few hours later, the supervisor's assistant went up the mountain to pass on a message, and found both men sitting on the porch, feet propped up on the railing, and both as "barefooted as a yard dog." Nobody gave Woody much trouble about shoes after that.

5. The median age in Atlanta is 31.5.

6. Georgia has a larger percentage of Indian place names still in use than any other state.

7. Don't blink when you pass through South Newport or you might miss the smallest church in America. At least, that's what they say. It seats twelve and was endowed by the inheritance of a local woman. It's open around the clock, but don't forget to turn off the lights when you leave.

8. The Cabbage Patch dolls were conceived and originate from a small town in North Georgia—Cleveland. In 1983, Cabbage Patch kids accounted for 98% of all dolls sold. Only Ken & Barbie can beat that.

9. Have another cookie. Juliette Gordon Low (Daisy Low) was born in Savannah 1860. She admired the Girl Guides in England and thought the United States should have an equivalent organization. In 1912, the first Girl Scouts met in genteel Savannah. Today, Girl Scouts can earn à merit badge just by showing up.

10. A group of Northern millionaires hired two experts to find the ideal vacation spot a century ago. They dismissed the French Riviera, Italy's shores, and other popular resorts of the day and finally chose Georgia's Golden Isles. J.P. Morgan, William Rockefeller, William Vanderbilt, Joseph Pulitzer, Astors, Armours, Cranes, Goodyears, Macys and more all flocked South.

11. Ouch. Before 1842, anesthetics were pretty primitive. But that year in Jefferson, Dr. Crawford W. Long performed the first operation using ether as an anesthetic.

12. It's a peach of a ride. The world's largest manufacturer of school buses is the Blue Bird Company in Macon.

13. Four percent of its land area is owned by the federal government.

14. There are 61 streets in Atlanta with the word "peachtree" in their names.

15. Christ Church in Frederica is featured in the first book of Eugenia Price's St. Simons Trilogy "Beloved Invader."

16. When does a pound of pork weigh less than a pound? Fincher's barbecue from Macon was the first barbecue to go into space. Astronaut Sonny Carter took it aboard the space shuttle with him on November 22, 1989.

17. Georgia, with an area of 59,441 square miles, is the 24th largest U.S. state and the biggest in land area east of the Mississippi River.

18. Waycross has an annual PogoFest every fall to celebrate Walt Kelly's comic strip characters who live in the swamp.

19. The Okefenokee National Wildlife Refuge was established in 1937 to preserve the swamp's valuable ecosystem. It encompasses 396,000 acres of the 438,000 acre Okefenokee Swamp. On a good day, you'll see alligators, sandhill cranes, osprey and many more varieties of marsh and wading birds here.

20. Athens has seven labyrinths, special energy spots created by water coming out of the earth. A dowsing rod is used to find and map the labyrinths, and believers walk the labyrinth and meditate. Three more labyrinths are scheduled for completion soon.

21. Beautiful marble is found on the Piedmont Plateau north of Atlanta. The state is the second leading supplier of marble in the country, and the Abraham Lincoln monument in Washington, D.C. is sculpted of Georgia marble.

22. Just when you think you know what Georgia looks like, the landscape will change. Georgia encompasses parts of six geographical regions. In the south, you'll find sections of the Atlantic Coastal Plain and the East Gulf Coastal Plain.

In the north you'll see the Piedmont Plateau region, an area of rolling hills, and three different regions of the Appalachian Mountains: the Blue Ridge, the Valley and Ridge region, and a section of the Cumberland Plateau in the northwest corner.

23. Bill Elliot, NASCAR driver, is a native of Dawsonville. This mountain town is also known as the Moonshine Capital of the state—Scots-Irish settlers brought their knowledge of distilling spirits from the old country. There may be a connection between driving fast and hauling moonshine out of the mountains, but don't bet on it.

24. There are no natural lakes in the peach state, but many rivers have been dammed to make large bodies of water for recreational use. These include Lake Seminole, Walter F. George Lake, and Lake Sidney Lanier, on the Chattahoochee River; Lake Sinclair, on the Oconee River; Hartwell and Strom Thurmond lakes, on the Savannah River; and Allatoona Lake, on the Etowah River. Parts of some lakes are in neighboring states.

25. It's a wild place. The wildlife includes many deer, raccoon, opossum, fox and squirrel, and some black bear in the mountains and the southeastern forest. Ducks, geese, and quail are plentiful, as are songbirds such as the mockingbird and wood thrush. Georgia's freshwater rivers and lakes are jumping with bass, bream, trout, perch, crappie and catfish. The state's coastal marine waters are teeming with crabs, oysters, shrimp and shad.

26. Native Americans aren't the only ones who find Sapelo Island intriguing. Fifty years ago, R.J. Reynolds was the last in a succession of millionaires to own the island. Fortunately, he was interested in marine research, and invited University of Georgia faculty to set up a place to work in an old dairy barn at his South End estate. This was the first time research was concentrated on marshland ecology anywhere in the world, and resulted in the creation of the University of Georgia's Marine Institute in 1950.

27. Theodore Roosevelt's mother, Mittie Bulloch Roosevelt, grew up in Roswell.

28. The South is steamy, and Georgia is no exception. Its location in the south, relatively low elevation, and proximity to the warm waters of the Atlantic and Gulf of Mexico make long hot summers, short mild winters and regular rainfall a pretty sure thing.

29. Albany is known as the Pecan and Candy Cane Capital of the world.

30. How cold does it get? The record low temperature was captured near Rome in 1940: minus 17 degrees Fahrenheit. The record high was recorded at Louisville in 1952: 112 degrees Fahrenheit.

31. Stone Mountain, east of Atlanta, is one of the largest known single masses of exposed granite in the world.

32. The Coastal Plain region has plentiful deposits of kaolin, a high-grade white clay. It breaks all the records as Georgia's largest export item. The rare clay, found only in the U.S. and China, is used to make fine china like Limoges and Wedgewood.

33. Much of the state's soil has a reddish tint because of its high clay content.

34. Democrats have held the governorship continuously in the state since 1872.

35. The average population density in 1990 was 109 people per square mile. This figure doesn't include coon dogs, aliens, cats or other approximations of human life.

36. The Bethesda Orphans Home, near Savannah, is the oldest orphanage in the United States, founded in 1740.

37. Take a boat to Sapelo Island and see the largest shell midden found in North America. It's a 6-foot high ring of oyster shells left by Native Americans centuries ago, used for purposes we can only guess at. Then again, maybe it's just their trash heap.

38. 2/3 of Georgia is covered with forests.

39. Elton John has been named as an honorary native of Atlanta. The flamboyant rock star has a home in the city.

40. Georgia has 95 institutions of higher education, with a combined annual enrollment of about 239,200 students. These institutions included the University of Georgia, at Athens, and Emory University, Georgia Institute of Technology, and Georgia State University, all at Atlanta. Pretty smart city.

41. Andersonville is the only national park to serve as a memorial to all Americans ever held as prisoners of war. It is also a National Historic Site, where thousands of Union soldiers were held captive during the Civil War.

42. Georgia has 23 covered bridges standing, one of which is reputed to house ghosts.

43. Jimmy Carter, a one-term governor (1971-75), became in 1976 the first native Georgian to win election to the U.S. presidency.

44. Ted Turner, Atlanta native, owns all rights to the MGM film "Gone With The Wind."

45. President Franklin D. Roosevelt's "Little White House" is in Warm Springs. He was known to children in the area as "Uncle Rosey." He built the only home he ever owned in Warm Springs at a cost of $8,738.14 and that was where he died.

46. Georgia's best-known sports event is the Masters, a golf tournament held at Augusta every April.

47. In the early 1990s the state had 196 AM and 184 FM radio broadcasting stations and 46 television stations. The state's first radio station, WSB, began operation in Atlanta in 1922.

48. Malcolm X's mentor, Nation of Islam leader Elijah Mohammed, was born Robert Poole in Washington County.

49. The oldest newspaper was the *Chronicle,* first published in Augusta in 1785.

50. Georgia is represented in the U.S. Congress by two senators and eleven representatives. The state has thirteen electoral votes in presidential elections.

51. Many runaway slaves fled to freedom in the Okefenokee Swamp. Moonshiners, too, found the forbidding, mysterious swamp a good place for hiding out.

52. The B-52s, an internationally-known pop rock group, are from Athens.

53. Waynesboro is the Bird Dog Capital of the World.

54. Nuts to you—Georgia typically leads all states in peanut and pecan production.

55. While all Cherokees were supposed to have been escorted out of Georgia via the Trail of Tears, some Cherokees remained as slaves for the white settlers and others simply disappeared into the mountains. As late as 1971, Cherokees were found in Georgia living in the wild, descendants of those who evaded the tragic forced migration of the early 19th century.

56. Communities of free men and women of color have existed in Georgia from Colonial times on.

57. The earliest known European settlement in Georgia was the Spanish mission of Santa Catalina, established in 1566 on Saint Catherines Island. The mission was overrun in 1680 by the British and their Native American allies.

58. Georgia contains more than 9000 manufacturing establishments, which together are responsible for the employment of over 500,000 workers.

59. In the early 1990s, more than 32 million travelers visited Georgia each year, and the state annually earned over $10 billion from tourism. The major tourist attractions of Georgia include the mountains of the northern part of the state, the Atlanta area, and the Atlantic coast.

60. Savannah is one of the oldest cities in the United States.

61. The James "Sloppy" Floyd State Park is named after a popular state representative. His football coach gave him the nickname, and he apparently could never quite shake it. A building in Atlanta also bears his name, including his nickname. He died in 1974.

62. If you feel like driving, there's plenty of room. You'll find about 109,600 miles of federal, state, and local roads, including 11,200 miles of interstate highway system.

63. Atlanta's William B. Hartsfield International Airport is one of the busiest in the nation.

64. Sea Island dwellers are often called "Geechee" after the local Ogeechee River.

65. The hedges lining the University of Georgia's football field in Athens have been there since 1929.

66. The mystique of Cumberland Island has been protected from development since 1972 when it was established as a national seashore. Only 300 visitors per day are allowed on the island, one of Georgia's barrier islands.

67. The major Native American groups in Georgia at the time of European settlement were the Lower Creeks and the Cherokees, both of which had well-established cultures.

68. Okra seeds were originally brought to this country from Africa, and the vegetable is popular in low-country cuisine today.

69. What do you do with more gold than you can handle? Build a mint, of course. There was so much gold being produced in the North Georgia region that the Federal government built a mint in Dahlonega in 1838. Six million dollars in gold coins were produced before the mint was closed in 1861. The rush ended in 1849, when word of gold in California reached Georgia and many of the miners headed west with visions of a bigger fortune dancing in their dreams.

70. During National Peanut Month in 1989, the Penta Hotel in Atlanta built one of the world's largest peanut butter & jelly sandwiches—15 foot by 10 foot, using 500 pounds of peanut butter and 200 pounds of jelly. They've changed their name to the Renaissance Atlanta Hotel Downtown, but still like to celebrate big. In 1993, they created the world's largest Easter Egg, and one of the world's largest chocolate bunnies in 1996.

71. The British seized Savannah in 1778, but they evacuated the state in 1782. Guerrilla fighters prevented them from ever gaining control of the interior.

72. In the beginning, Georgia claimed practically all of what is now Mississippi and much of Alabama, and granted this territory to private land companies. These grants (the Yazoo Land Frauds) were declared invalid in 1800 by the U.S. Congress.

73. Savannah is the largest foreign commerce port on the South Atlantic Coast and the farthest inland port on the East Coast.

74. The Southern Christian Leadership Conference, a major civil rights organization, makes its head-quarters in Atlanta.

75. Georgia's original people—Native Americans—started their day with a cup of strong, black, caffeinated beverage. Their staples were corn, squash and beans—all basics of Southern cooking today. But their matrilineal society was far from being traditional in the South. Most social structures were organized around women, like practices in marriage and child-rearing, and women had a strong voice in decision-making.

76. Georgia is the third-largest peach producing state in the nation.

77. Romance was in the air at Cumberland Island on September 22, 1996. John Kennedy chose the wild and beautiful island as the perfect wedding site.

78. The rock group REM is from Athens.

79. In 1964, Georgia for the first time since the Civil War cast its electoral votes for a Republican presidential candidate. George C. Wallace, running as the nominee of the American Independent party, carried the state in 1968.

80. The Athens Transit System ("The Bus") has been ranked number one in America among systems its size. UGA students ride for free, since the fare is covered under their transportation fee.

81. Ol' Man River in Georgia may be headed east or south. Some rivers flow to the Atlantic Ocean; others flow to the Gulf of Mexico.

82. In 1943, Georgia became the first state to give 18-year-olds the vote. Twenty-eight years later, it became a federal right.

83. In Brunswick, you can find Lover's Oak at the intersection of Albany and Prince Streets on the south end of town. It's 900 years old and the subject of many local legends; Native American maidens and warriors used to meet under its protective boughs.

84. Macon has more than 224,000 flowering cherry trees. During their annual Cherry Blossom Festival, the city gives away 7,500-10,000 trees to anyone in the county. Macon is officially the Cherry Blossom Capital of the world, as recorded in the Congressional Record.

85. Go fish. Towns County has 200 miles of trout streams.

86. Ever hear of world-famous Georgia silk? When a group of enterprising businessmen tried to establish a silk industry in the area they created the town of Canton, about a mile east of Etowah in Cherokee County, named after the China silk capital. The industry never really took off.

87. Otis Redding was born in Dawson on September 9, 1941. His family moved to Macon when he was three, and by his mid-teens Otis had left school and started working odd jobs to help support his family.

88. Leading agricultural products include broiler chickens, chicken eggs, peanuts, corn, soybeans, and cattle. Georgia usually ranks with Arkansas and Alabama as the top three U.S. producers of broiler chickens

89. Only about 1/10 of Georgia's 100-mile outer seashore is developed.

90. Long before European settlers arrived, Creek and Cherokee Indians called the rolling hills, gentle plains and rugged mountains of Georgia home. Native Americans had no conception of "owning" land, but they still fought for control of the territory many times. In Cherokee County, there's a town called Ballground that is significant to this tradition. The oral history of both tribes describe "Taliwa," which was either a ball game, lacrosse, or a battle that took place here probably in the mid 1700's, possibly 1755.

91. Hernando De Soto was motivated primarily by gold when he explored the North Georgia area in the early 1540s. He heard reports that Native Americans were successfully panning for gold along the Chattahoochee River north of Atlanta. Before long, Spanish miners came to work alongside them, and established small settlements which thrived until the early 18th century.

92. There's always something to celebrate in Georgia. In the Northeast Mountains alone, you'll find Blairsville's Sorghum Festival, Dahlonega's Gold Rush Days and Old-Fashioned Christmas, Gainesville's Mule Camp Market, Lake Lanier Islands' Great Pumpkin Festival, Hiawassee's Rhododendron Festival and Georgia Mountain Fair, Cornelia's Big Red Apple Festival and Clarkesville's Mountain Laurel Festival, just to name a few.

93. Life is tough when you're a billionaire. Henry Ford was looking for a place to get away from the pressures of his automobile kingdom nearly 75 years ago, and he built Richmond Hill Plantation. He also bought some 85,000 acres of land and put up 292 residential and community buildings, including schools, churches, a store, a sawmill and a medical clinic. This community became Richmond Hill.

94. The first Native American newspaper was published by Joseph Sequoyah in New Echota, historic capital of the Cherokee Nation which was established in 1828. *The Cherokee Phoenix* first rolled off the presses on February 21,1828, and had an immediate international circulation. The paper was published until May 31, 1834.

95. Dean Rusk, Secretary of State under John Fitzgerald Kennedy, grew up in Cherokee County. Authorities have named a middle school in his honor near his family's old home.

96. Newt Gingrich graduated from Baker High School in Columbus in 1962. He represents Georgia's 6th Congressional District in the House of Representatives, where he's currently serving his 10th term. He's the only Republican to be reelected as Speaker of the House since 1928. He lives in Marietta.

97. Much of the Okefenokee Swamp remains unexplored.

98. In 1860, the vast majority of farms in Georgia—31,000—were no more than 100 acres. Most functioned without slave labor. Now, Georgia has about 51,000 farms, averaging about 265 acres.

99. Folks in Georgia can be fiercely independent. The people of Cherokee and Pickens Counties were staunch supporters of the Union during the Civil War, even though the rebels won several initial battles. That made it even more of a shock when Sherman ordered the town of Canton burned in October, 1864.

100. If you have a taste for wild pig, call the Savannah National Wildlife Refuge. They hold deer, feral hog, and squirrel hunts during the fall and winter to keep the population manageable.

101. Only one written language has ever been developed by a single person. From 1821-33, Georgia native Joseph Sequoyah struggled to develop a method for Cherokees to communicate in writing. He named the language "Talking Leaves," a satirical note on the Native American perception of whites. The Cherokee felt that the white man's words dried up and blew away like leaves when the words no longer suited them.

102. Gold proved to be the downfall of the Cherokees in Georgia. They controlled most of the land where gold could be found, so it was decided that they must be removed. This eventually led to the Trail of Tears. "Dahlonega" means "yellow metal" in Cherokee.

103. A small colony of refugees from the French Revolution settled the town of Chocolate on Sapelo Island.

104. At the Amicalola Falls State Park, you can see falls higher than Niagara, but they are much narrower. They are also the tallest falls east of the Mississippi. "Amicalola" is Cherokee for tumbling water.

105. What's left of the vast bottomlands on Georgia's coast is contained within the Savannah National Wildlife Refuge, and you can still see the southern bald eagle soaring majestically overhead.

106. In the Piedmont National Wildlife Refuge, you're likely to spot the red cockaded woodpecker. This bird has more highly developed family values than many other species. It nests in family groups or clans, and male offspring from the previous year often remain to help feed the new nestlings. The old trees in this pine forest refuge meet the habitat needs of this endangered species.

107. There is a mysterious stone wall at the top of a mountain in North Georgia. It was built between 500 B.C. and 1500 A.D. and ranges in height from two to six feet. It was probably higher when it was first built. Archeologists are puzzled about who built it and why, and theories abound. One theory says it was built for religious reasons, while another ascribes the structure to the equally mysterious Welsh prince Madoc, who landed in Mobile Bay around 1400 A.D. and headed north. You can see the wall for yourself at Fort Mountain State Park.

108. Georgia Governor Joseph E. Brown felt so strongly about states' rights that he kicked out Federal troops at Fort Pulaski before Georgia officially seceded from the Union. Then, during the Civil War, he even threatened to secede from the Confederacy.

109. The citizens of Dahlonega presented the state with a gift of gold in 1958. After being pounded into thin sheets, the precious metal was attached to the top of the State House in Atlanta. The gold dome is a landmark today, a lasting symbol to our nation's first gold rush.

110. Head north to Rabun Gap and you'll find an authentic working grist mill, located on a private waterfall in the beautiful Wolf Fork Valley area of Rabun County. It's also an antique-filled three bedroom country inn. Sleepwalking is not advised.

111. Edwin Booth, Lillie Langtry, Oscar Wilde, John Philip Sousa, Will Rogers and Booker T. Washington all appeared on the stage of the Springer Opera House in Columbus. Now restored to its original glory, it serves as Georgia's official State Theatre.

112. There is a grain of truth to the coastal folklore celebrating slaves who "walked back to Africa." An Ebo leader from Nigeria got off a slave ship and led his people into the sea rather than submitting to slavery. It happened on St. Simons Island, but every island has its own Ebo's Landing, where the spirits of the Africans are said to reside.

113. In the mid-60s, Lady Astor called Savannah "a beautiful lady with a dirty face." Now, Savannah has more than 1,000 homes restored in a 3.3 square mile area, one of the largest, most handsome urban historic districts in the country.

114. People in Calvary are stubborn about having a little fun in the fall. Mule Days in Calvary begin on the first Saturday in November. Events include mule judging in ten categories, a mule parade, and a tobacco spitting contest.

115. Lake Lanier recreational facility is the most popular in the entire U.S. Army Engineers' network, more heavily visited than any other in the U.S. It's also the largest inland marina in the country.

116. On the island of St. Marys, spooky old Oak Grove Cemetery's marble markers are inscribed in French on the graves of Acadians who were banished with Evangeline in 1755. Henry Wadsworth Longfellow immortalized the sad tale of Evangeline in his poem of the same name published in 1847. She was separated from her lover Gabriel and spent the rest of her life looking for him. Finally, she became a Sister of Mercy in Philadelphia, Pennsylvania. There, in an almshouse, she found Gabriel as he was dying.

117. Maybe they should call it "The Granite State." Georgia is the nation's leading supplier of granite.

GORGEOUS GEORGIA

118. Eugene O'Neil wrote his only comedy in a house he named Casa Genotta on Sea Island. Titled 'Ah, Wilderness!' and published in 1933, it's a nostalgic view of small-town life.

119. Over 150 different varieties of wildflowers have been identified at Providence Canyon, where there are 16 huge ravines, some 1/2 mile long and 300 feet wide, falling to a depth of 160 feet.

120. At the turn of the century, a pencil manufacturer bought Little St. Simons Island intending to harvest its many cedar trees. But the cedar was too twisted to use, and the owner kept the island for his family to use a vacation retreat. It's the last family-owned barrier island in Georgia.

121. In 1972, Andrew Young of Atlanta was elected the first black congressman from the South since Reconstruction.

122. The highest state park in Georgia is Black Rock Mountain. This gem is buried on the Eastern Continental Divide in the northeast corner of the state.

123. Habitat for Humanity is Georgia-based and originated from a small farming commune near Plains. Millard and Linda Fuller were members of the Christian commune in 1976 when they developed the idea of building houses for families who otherwise would never be able to afford their own homes. It's now an international project, with its most visible volunteer being the former President Jimmy Carter.

124. Savannah is home to one of the world's largest pulp mills.

125. Abac, Georgia, is one of the first places listed in the US Postal Service ZIP Code Directory.

126. The Georgia Guidestones near Elberton are known as the"Stonehenge of America." Erected in 1980, no one knows who commissioned the work. There are four upright stones, one center stone and two cap stones, in addition to the support stones. They stand 19 feet tall. Each stone is inscribed with a guide to conservation and preservation of the earth and humankind in twelve languages.

127. George Washington was a house guest in Savannah. As a "thank you" gift for the city's hospitality, he sent the city a pair of bronze cannons he captured at Yorktown.

128. An acre of marsh in the Golden Isles could provide 1/2 billion dollars in shellfish over a 25-year period.

129. Atlanta, founded in 1837, was originally named Terminus. It was a vital railroad freight center.

130. Gascoigne Bluff is a popular spot. Overlooking the Frederica River, it was first a Native American campground. Then in the 1500s, Franciscans built a monastery nearby. Later, during colonial days, the landing at the bluff became the state's first naval base. It was during this time that it acquired the name it has today. It was named after the man who first surveyed the Georgia coast for England.

When the Spanish fleet sailed up from St. Augustine, they landed here.

During the plantation era, sea island cotton was shipped to ports around the world from the Hamilton Plantation dock at Gascoigne. Exports stopped during the Civil War when the bluff became U. S. Naval Head.

131. Georgia is the nation's leading textile producer.

132. Atlanta locals like to tell visitors that Atlanta's winding confusing streets follow old cow paths and Native American trails. It's notoriously easy to get lost in Atlanta.

133. Jekyll Island, playground of millionaires around the turn of the century, was purchased by the state of Georgia in 1947 for $675,000, including all the buildings, tennis courts and assorted attractions.

134. When other people said Georgia pine was useless, Dr. Charles H. Herty didn't believe them. This industrial chemist born in Milledgeville discovered how to make newsprint from fast growing pines. Now, Kraft paper, fine white paper, cellulose and plastics are possible because of his research.

135. Over 1/2 of the state is owned by pulpwood and lumber companies.

136. In 1864, the Battle of Atlanta destroyed 99% of the city. The smoldering chimneys of houses and businesses were often all that remained, and these stark landmarks earned the nickname of "Sherman's Sentinels."

137. The Fernbank Science Center in Atlanta is home to the only planetarium in the US owned by a public school system. It's the third largest planetarium in the world.

138. Scottish Highlanders settled in Darien and introduced golf to the New World in this little fishing village. The first of the McIntosh clan arrived in 1736 and there is still a strong Scottish influence today.

139. Atlanta is ranked number 2 behind New York City as a computer city. Computer job growth is expected to be high over the next few years.

140. Atlanta is second only to Chicago in space devoted to shopping areas.

141. Savannah has the second largest St. Patrick's Day celebration in the country, second only to New York. They've been celebrating it for more than 164 years. Twenty-five percent of Savannah's population is of Irish descent.

142. The constitution of 1877 limited state appropriations to elementary schools and the university. It was 1910 before a constitutional amendment allowed taxes to be levied for high schools. Georgia's current state constitution was ratified in 1983.

143. Tallulah Gorge near Clayton is the deepest canyon in the United States besides the Grand Canyon. It was a popular destination for turn-of-the-century Atlantans.

144. The East's southernmost ski run is in Sky Valley. They receive 7-10 inches of snow every year.

145. Sing "hallelujah." John Wesley wrote the first English hymnal in Savannah in 1736 while he was rector of Christ Church.

146. The Tubman African American Museum in Macon is Georgia's largest African-American museum. The museum is home to a nationally-known mural titled "From Africa to America;" 75 feet long, it depicts the history of African-Americans over the centuries.

147. Gainesville, Georgia, is the Poultry Capital of the world, processing about 2,850,000 million broilers a week.

148. The diversity and richness of the Okefenokee swamp is not duplicated anywhere else on earth.

149. Piedmont Plateau is named from an Italian word that means "foot of the mountain." European settlers noted the region's resemblance to Southern Europe.

150. Prehistoric sharks' teeth can still be found in the sand dunes along the Flint River south of Albany. The region used to be part of an ancient sea.

151. According to legend, the Indian nations agreed that no wars would be fought on the lush sub-tropical barrier islands along Georgia's coast. They all pledged that tribal members would visit there only in a spirit of friendship.

152. In the Confederate prison at Andersonville, 13,000 Union soldiers died. At the end of the war, the commandant was tried for wartime atrocities, convicted and hung on the spot.

153. Chickamauga and Chattanooga National Military Park was established in 1890 and became the nation's first military park. It was the site of the Civil War's bloodiest battle—30,000 casualties.

154. Telfair Mansion and Art Museum in Savannah is the South's oldest public art museum.

155. The Fox Theater in Atlanta, built in 1928 as a Shrine Temple, is second only to Radio City Music Hall in New York in size. The Moller Organ is one of the world's largest theater pipe organs.

156. Ellison's Cave in North Georgia is the deepest cave east of the Mississippi.

157. Savannah is home to the third oldest Jewish congregation in the United States, Temple Mickve Israel.

GORGEOUS GEORGIA 

158. Georgia is the 7th fastest growing state in the nation. Must be all that rain and hot weather.

159. DeKalb Farmers' Market in Atlanta houses 140,000 square feet of exotic fruit, cheeses, seafood, sausages, breads and delicacies from around the world.

160. Wild horses on the barrier islands are probably the descendants of those left by Spanish explorers in the 17th century.

161. The SS Savannah set sail from Savannah in 1819, the first steamship to cross the ocean.

162. The white-tailed deer is now Georgia's most abundant large mammal.

163. Sea Island is one of only 13 five-star resorts in the United States.

GORGEOUS GEORGIA

164. The Right Whale only calves off of the Georgia coast. It's picky, but it has a right to be—there are only 350 left in the world.

165. Crime is likely to be hazardous to your health in Kennesaw. The city responded to gun-control legislation by requiring that every household own a gun.

166. Three of the four most interesting archeological sites east of the Rockies are in Georgia: the aboriginal earthworks at Ocmulgee Mounds near Macon, Kolomoki Mounds in Southwest Georgia, and Etowah Mounds in Northwest Georgia. Etowah Mounds is among the most important finds in North America, with some artifacts dating back 10,000 years.

167. The French were the first to discover the beauty of Georgia's barrier islands.

168. When De Soto came through Georgia in 1540, he exposed the native populations to European diseases to which they had no immunity. A short time later, up to 3/4 of the Southeastern native population was wiped out by influenza, smallpox and other illnesses.

169. The communities flooded in 1957 to create Lake Lanier still exist under millions of gallons of water. Farmhouses, churches, a race track, even an 18-hole golf course can be explored by divers. The lake was formed when Buford Dam was completed.

170. What does a multi-millionaire give his wife for her birthday? Thomas Carnegie bought Cumberland Island as a birthday gift for his wife over 100 years ago. Now, it's about the last place of any size you can go on the East Coast that is relatively undeveloped and isolated.

171. The first experimental garden in the US was in Savannah in 1733. Work done here showed early farmers that the state was perfect for growing cotton and peaches, two crops that would shape Georgia's history and culture.

172. There are over 1200 international businesses operating in Atlanta. Thirty-one foreign trade and tourism offices operate there, and 28 foreign chambers of commerce.

173. *Gone With The Wind* sold more than a million copies in the first six months after publication in 1936. It has been published in 70 different languages. Frankly, Scarlett, that's a serious best seller.

174. Eighty percent of the US population lives within two hours of the Atlanta airport, which is the second busiest in the nation.

175. At 186 feet, Toccoa Falls in North Georgia is some 19 feet higher than Niagara Falls.

176. Cloudland Canyon, a state park in the northwest corner, is affectionately known as Georgia's "Little Grand Canyon." It was virtually unknown and inaccessible until the 1930s, when roads were first built in the area.

177. Mt. Yonah is Georgia's foremost rock-climbing area. Even the Army Rangers agree that it's tough—they use it for a training ground. "Yonah" means "bear" in Cherokee.

178. The Stovall Covered Bridge is Georgia's smallest covered bridge, built around 1895. It was built using the Kingpost design, and is one span wide and 33 feet long. The bridge was featured in the movie, "I'd Climb the Highest Mountain".

179. The official colors of Georgia are green and peach.

180. The island of Ossabaw, privately owned but managed by the state as a heritage preserve, had a problem with donkey overpopulation. They solved it by giving the jackasses vasectomies.

181. The average backpack taken on the Appalachian Trail weighs fifty pounds. At Suches, the first road crossing 20 miles north of the trail's beginning, the postmaster is busy sending packages of gear home that backpackers have decided they don't really need to carry on the long journey. It takes about six months to hike the entire trail, and costs between $4,000-$5,000 for supplies, equipment, and postage.

182. Coca-Cola was originally marketed as a headache and hangover tonic.

183. When cotton went bust as a cash crop and folks in South Georgia had to find a new source of income, one native said "we soon discovered one Yankee was worth two bales of cotton and was twice as easy to pick." Even today, massive plantations cater to wealthy Northerners who fly South to avoid harsh winter weather.

184. The lighthouse on St. Simons is one of the oldest continuously working lighthouses in the country. Operated by the U.S. Coast Guard, its light is visible for 18 miles out to sea.

185. During the winter of 1892-93, Jekyll Island Club records show that hunters brought in 1787 quail, 34 ducks, seven wild hogs, 23 marsh hens, 40 doves, 20 woodcocks, 24 raccoons, 14 deer, nine pheasants and five alligators. This was a typical season, lasting three months. Hope they were hungry.

186. East of Montezuma is a community of about 100 Mennonite families. They've lived in Georgia since 1954, their traditional clothes and lifestyle similar to the Amish except for their acceptance of modern machinery.

187. At the National Country Music Museum in Buena Vista, you can have a gander at Linda Ronstadt's satin jogging shorts, Tanya Tucker's boots, Johnny Cash's complete bedroom suite and more.

188. If caviar's your passion, you belong in Darien. One of the largest female sturgeons ever caught was netted in the Darien River. It weighed 496 pounds and gave up 100 pounds of roe. That's fish eggs to back-country folks.

189. In the 1730s, John Wesley established the first Sunday School in the New World at his church, Christ Church in Savannah.

190. The Center for Disease Control is in Atlanta, the only federal agency not headquartered in Washington D.C. Nobody knows if they're more efficient because of it.

191. Georgia's Atlantic shoreline is 115 miles long. But if you took out all the twists, turns, coils and doubling-back around the coast and estuarine waters, it would actually stretch for a total of 2,344 linear miles—ten times longer than the French and Italian Riverias combined.

192. In 1867, Atlanta University was founded, the first of six schools dedicated to the education of former slaves.

193. The premier site for hang-gliding on the East Coast is the Lookout Mountain Flight Park on McCarty Bluff.

194. Pickett's Mill Battlefield is one of the best preserved Civil War battlefields in the country. The battle was fought in 1864.

195. The Confederate Memorial on the north face of Stone Mountain is the largest sculpture in the world. It features Confederate heroes Robert E. Lee, Jefferson Davis and Stonewall Jackson. The sculpture was begun in 1923 and not completed until 1970.

196. Brunswick stew, traditionally a savory concoction of wild game and vegetables, may have been the culinary creation of 18th century fur traders in Brunswick. Virginia lays claim to the creation of Brunswick stew also, and the two states have an annual cook-off to see who does it better.

197. The Wright brothers started their flying school in Augusta in 1910.

198. How did Scarlett get to be the woman we all know and love? She attended Fayetteville Academy, built in 1855. Although the woman is a fictional creation, her school is a very real institution.

199. President William Taft once kept a large crowd waiting to hear him speak while he polished off his last —and 11th—waffle in an Oglethorpe Avenue dining room in Savannah.

200. The red cedar was sacred to the Cherokee. They would not allow it to be used as firewood, and carved religious objects from the sweet-smelling wood instead.

201. Many Appalachian settlers were loyal to the Crown during the Revolution. Generations later, some also refused to fight for the Confederacy during the Civil War.

202. Augusta has the first black Baptist congregation in America, organized in 1787. Their current sanctuary was built in 1801. Presumably the second oldest black congregation was founded in Savannah in 1788.

203. Cypress trees occupy 4/5 of the Okefenokee Swamp. The massive trees grow equally well in water or in land.

204. While the city of Rome, Georgia may be surrounded by seven hills just like its sister city in Italy, it might as easily have been called "Hamburg," "Warsaw", "Pittsburgh," or "Hillsboro." The city fathers couldn't decide so they threw all these options into a hat and drew out the winner —"Rome."

205. The late Jackie Kennedy escaped to Thomasville after John F. Kennedy's assassination.

206. Margaret Mitchell, author of *Gone with The Wind*, affectionately called her home in midtown Atlanta "the Dump." It's still there, and still looks pretty rough around the edges. Also in midtown is the intersection of Peachtree and Thirteenth Streets, where a taxi struck Mitchell in 1949, killing her. She was 49 years old. She's buried in Atlanta's Oakland Cemetery.

207. In 1780, Washington, Georgia became the first municipality to be named after George Washington. It is also the home of the first female newspaper editor in the U.S., Sarah Hillhouse. She became editor of the Washington Monitor when her husband, the previous editor, died in 1803.

208. The tower on top of 4,784 foot Brasstown Bald in North Georgia provides a 360-degree panorama of four different states.

209. In Mountain City, on top of the Blue Ridge Divide, water runs off in two directions—some goes east to the Atlantic, while some goes south to the Gulf of Mexico.

210. Fort Gordon's Signal Corps operation in Augusta ranks as one of the largest communications and electronics training center in the world.

211. Watson Mill Bridge near Comer is one of the longest covered bridges still standing in Georgia.

212. Woodrow Wilson moved to Augusta when he was one year old, in 1857. When he received his law degree in 1882, he set up a law practice in Atlanta. It was a struggle to gain clients, though, so he soon gave it up and embarked on the academic career that would eventually lead to his political career. The income tax was created during Wilson's administration.

213. The bell in the slave market of Louisville was cast in France in 1772 at the request of the King, then shipped as his gift to a New Orleans convent. It was captured by pirates en route, sold in Savannah, and ended up in Louisville. The market was built in 1758.

214. The 1815 Davenport House triggered the Savannah restoration movement in the 1950s when the city proposed tearing the old house down to make room for a parking lot.

215. Atlanta has more BMW owners per capita than any other city in the United States.

216. In the isolated mountain regions of Georgia, it's still possible to hear old ballads sung in Elizabethan English—songs handed down from generation to generation in their original form.

GORGEOUS GEORGIA

217. It's easy to recognize a good thing when you see it. Native Americans appreciated the vacation potential of St. Simons Island hundreds of years ago. When General James Oglethorpe arrived from England to settle Georgia, they were here. Georgia was the thirteenth colony, settled in 1733.

218. At one time, Augusta was one of the busiest cotton ports in the world. Cotton bales crowded so densely around the cotton exchange that local kids could jump from one bale to another without landing on the sidewalk for more than a mile.

219. Columbus, on the western side of the state, was the final city to be settled in the original 13 colonies. It's now Georgia's second largest city with a population of about 300,000.

220. Rome has three rivers running through its downtown area and seven historical districts.

221. Gold mining in Dahlonega and northeast Georgia remained profitable for decades, until the price of gold was fixed in the early twentieth century.

222. Called "Terminus," then "Marthasville" in honor of Governor Lumpkin's daughter, Atlantans today should be glad of the name change. Can you imagine being called a "Marthasvillian?"

223. Mary Dillard of Dillard, Georgia, treated British soldiers to a home-cooked feast during the Revolutionary War. While they ate, she slipped out and rode her horse pell-mell through the mountains to warn her husband's cavalry unit that the Redcoats were on their way.

224. Black bears are so prevalent in North Georgia that the Forest Service allows some hunting of the creatures every year.

225. Erskine Caldwell was born in Moreland in 1903. He wrote *God's Little Acre* and *Tobacco Road,* among other Southern classics. Moreland's other claim to fame is a hidden rise where cars allegedly roll uphill.

226. Tallulah Falls was a favorite honeymoon spot at the turn of the century. Mr. and Mrs. Bankhead honeymooned here, and later may have chosen the name "Tallulah" for their daughter because of the romantic associations. Or the noted entertainer may have been named after her grandmother—no one is quite sure. "Tallulah" means "awesome" in Cherokee.

227. A traveling minister was denied the right to preach in the lower market in Augusta. Outraged, he vowed disaster would befall the marketplace. In 1878 his prediction came true—a cyclone destroyed all but a single pillar.

228. Rock City, of "See Rock City" billboard fame, is typically associated with Chattanooga, Tennessee. But it is actually located in Georgia, where it was first called "Fairyland." Its original promoter, who plastered the Southeast with "See Rock City" signs painted on birdhouses, barns and practically any flat surface in the 1920s, also invented miniature golf.

229. The Chatooga River is the setting for James Dickey's novel *Deliverance*, which was also captured on film. Dickey calls the Chatooga "the most dangerous river in the country besides the Colorado." Actually, it's steeper than the Colorado, dropping 275 feet within a six-mile stretch. There are 48 major rapids along one three mile section, some with names like "Screamin' Left Turn," "Sock-Em-Dog," and "Corkscrew."

230. The average yearly precipitation is about 50 inches.

231. The Foxfire books were some of Doubleday's best selling books ever, a collection of the region's legends and lore. The Foxfire Museum is in Mountain City.

232. Howard Finster, noted "outsider" artist, started building his famous Paradise Gardens near Summerville in the 1940s.

233. Georgia's Northwest Mountains are a continuation of the Great Smokey Mountains, and are much younger than the Blue Ridge Mountains to the east.

234. Of the 198 minerals mined in Georgia, 50 of them are found in Bartow County, more than in any comparable place in the nation.

235. They know how to cut the rug in Dalton. Dalton is the Carpet Capital of the world, providing 65% of the world's carpet supply.

236. The little town of Ellijay and the surrounding area produces 400,000 bushels of apples every year.

237. Folks in Claxton like to know where their rattlesnakes are. The second weekend in March, they host a Rattlesnake Round-up, complete with long-distance runs, crafts, a parade, a Round-Up Queen, gospel and cloggers. For the creatures with no legs, the amusements are limited: there are hundreds of penned-up snakes caught in the surrounding area, and prizes are awarded for the biggest one. Fitzgerald also has a similar festival every year.

238. At the Wild Ridge and Myrtlewood plantations, a Thomasville lumber baron and land owner spends $10,000 annually to care for his hunting dogs. Both plantations accept overnight guests and the hunting, naturally, is said to be excellent.

239. The Masters Golf Tournament in Augusta is one of the best-known golf events in the world. It's held at the Augusta National Golf Course, which used to be one of the largest indigo plantations in the South. Its previous owner, Baron Julius Alphonse Beckmans, imported camellias from Japan, France, England, and Belgium, brought in amur privet from France, wisteria from Japan, Chinese Holly, 40 varieties of azaleas, 1300 varieties of pears, 900 strains of apples and 300 varieties of grapes. No one's going hungry on that golf course.

240. Berry College in Rome has the largest campus in the world. Berry College was originally founded as the Berry Schools for mountain children.

241. The Georgia Marble Company in the Tate-Jasper area runs one of the largest marble quarry operations in the world.

242. At the turn of the century, Lithia Springs was home to Sweetwater Park Hotel, one of the largest frame structures in the world. Astors, Whitneys, Mark Twain, Grover Cleveland, Joel Chandler Harris, President William McKinley—all were invited guests who believed in the water's curative powers. The hotel burned in 1912 and was never rebuilt.

243. Fortune magazine named Atlanta the #1 best city to do business in.

244. Quitman was known as the Smokehouse of the Confederacy during the Civil War. Even now, surrounding farms grow large quantities of corn and peanuts for fattening hogs, and farmers still cure and preserve meat just like they did more than a century ago.

245. Alice M. Birney, the founder of the first Parent-Teacher Association, was from Marietta.

246. The Ocmulgee Mounds are nearly three stories tall, and stretch the length of a football field. The dirt to build the mound was transported one basketful at a time.

247. Minerals found in the state include coal, sand and gravel, talc, soapstone, barite, manganese, and bentonite.

248. The 2,050 mile Appalachian Trail passes through 15 states, two national parks, and eight national forests. It begins at Springer Mountain in North Georgia.

249. Atlanta was the first major city in the South to elect a black mayor—Maynard H. Jackson was elected in 1977.

250. Atlanta is the only city in the United States ever to have been entirely leveled by war.

251. Atlanta's Flatiron Building with its distinctive triangular shape predates New York's Flatiron Building by five years. It was built in 1897.

252. During the Civil War, Albany was known as the Breadbasket of the Confederacy.

253. Georgia has the largest number of counties (139) of any state besides one. That state is, naturally, Texas.

254. Cairo is the Pickle Capital of the world. Roddenbery Pickles are made there.

255. The Cohutta Wilderness area in North Georgia is some of the wildest and most rugged country left in the eastern United States. Take your compass.

256. The Varsity in Atlanta, known for its chili dogs, shakes and fries, may be the world's largest drive-in. Are there any Rolaids in your glove box?

257. The Big Oak of Thomasville dates from 1685, stands 68 feet tall and has a limb spread of 155 feet. Its circumference is 22.7 feet, and it is listed on the National Register of Historic Places.

258. Henry Flipper was born in Thomasville in 1856 and is now buried there. Why give a flip? He was the first black man to be accepted to West Point.

259. Ola Barber Pittman must be related to Scarlett somehow. This spunky woman is the daughter of the man who co-founded the Coca-Cola bottling works near Valdosta, and she was so determined to save the neoclassical house he built at the turn of the century that she tied herself to a pillar to thwart the wrecking ball. It worked. The house is now the headquarters for the Chamber of Commerce in Valdosta.

260. The Lapham-Patterson House was built by C.W. Lapham, a Chicago shoe merchant. Not one room in the house is square or rectangular. The owner, a survivor of the Chicago Fire of 1871, incorporated fifty exits in his winter retreat, leading from the home to verandahs, balconies or the yard.

261. Pebble Hill Plantation, near Thomasville, is one of the most luxurious plantations in Georgia. At one time there were eighty servants in attendance here, and the property included two schoolhouses, a hospital for hunting dogs, a medical clinic, firehouse, cemetery, reflecting pool, formal gardens and stables. But the house is not an example of life in the old South—it was built, like so many plantations in South Georgia, by wealthy Northerners who were escaping from long icy winters around the turn of the century.

262. Valdosta has the winningest high school football program in national history.

263. Maybe everything's not so peachy in Atlanta after all. All those roads called "Peachtree" may be mistakenly named from a corruption of a Native American term for "pitch tree."

264. In the Thomasville area, seventy plantation owners control 300,000 acres of land.

265. Researchers in Tifton developed a new strain of hybrid grass that's hardy and great for cattle ranchers. Tifton grass covers no fewer than ten million acres in the South.

266. A little bit of Georgia can be found in millions of gardens across North America. Tomato, pepper, cabbage and onion seedlings grown in Tifton are shipped throughout the continent.

267. A century ago Valdosta was the wealthiest per capita city of its size in the United States. Nothing much has changed. Lowndes County, with Valdosta as its county seat, is still in the top 4%.

268. That's a great goober. On I-75 south of Ashburn is the world's largest peanut. It rests in the center of a golden crown, ten feet tall. The tower supporting it is 15 feet tall.

269. From the 1830s until the Civil War, Thomasville was the southernmost town in the United States served by the railroads.

270. William Cameron Forbes' plantation, where General Patton played polo, is now Thomas College. The rich still flock to the plantations around Thomasville, and it's estimated to cost $700,000 annually to keep one of these lavish spreads functioning smoothly.

GORGEOUS GEORGIA

271. If you say Cairo folks are sweet, you're not kidding. At one time, Cairo shipped more cane syrup than any other city in the nation.

272. The Atlanta Ballet is the nation's oldest existing regional ballet.

273. The York House in Mountain City is a historic inn that has been open continuously since 1896.

274. The Ritz-Carlton hotel chain is Atlanta-based and Atlanta-owned.

275. Andrew College, in Cuthbert, was founded in 1854. It is the second oldest institution in the United States chartered to confer degrees on women. Wesleyan College in Macon was chartered in 1836, and was the first college in the world for the education of women.

276. Cherokee legend held that warriors who ventured into the water at Tallulah Falls would never return.

277. The clock on the Wayne County Courthouse has been in operation for more than 90 years.

278. Thomasville first became well-known around 1870 as a place to take a tuberculosis cure. It was believed that the air was healthy and encourage recuperation from this highly contagious respiratory disease.

279. Some folks say Albany got its name when two workers were building a bridge across the Flint River. "That'll be all, Benny," hollered one to the other. You can still hear it pronounced that way.

280. The largest chemical cellulose-producing pulp mill in the world is in Jessup.

281. Jefferson Davis, President of the defeated Confederate States of America, was arrested in Ocilla near Irwinville by Federal forces in 1865. Officially, he was said to have been disguised in his wife's shawl, but some scholars dispute that.

282. Say Hallelujah and pass the snake. Old Lake Church, five miles east of Metter, is one of the oldest Primitive Baptist Churches in existence today. It was founded in 1823.

283. The Ladson Genealogical Library in Vidalia is nationally known, and contains a wealth of information not available anywhere else in the world.

284. If you drive through McRae you might think you've accidentally landed in New York. They have a Statue of Liberty on display, but she's only 1/12 actual size. The town had her built to commemorate Lady Liberty's 100th birthday.

285. Zoo Atlanta is one of the top ten zoos in the United States. It's home to nearly 1,000 animals. They have one of the largest collections of gorillas, numbering 19, with eight born since 1988. In good Southern tradition, all the babies have been reared by their mothers.

286. Doc Holliday, Wyatt Earp's sidekick at the OK Corral, was a native of South Georgia's plantation region.

287. Claxton is the Fruitcake Capital of the World. They're not referring to the locals, either. They bake 85,000 pounds of fruitcake every day.

288. The Peach Blossom Trail links 11 communities in eight counties along Highway 341. Orchards line the road, and a 25 foot lighted peach on a 100 foot pole helps dispel any lingering doubts about the nature of the fruit harvested here.

289. Who says farming isn't the sweet life? The famed Vidalia onion, of Vidalia, Georgia and surrounding areas, has more natural sugar than an orange. Raising and selling these prized vegetables is strictly controlled and is a $30 million industry. Vidalia has a high incidence of UFO sightings, too, but there's no evidence that these two facts are related.

290. A visitor described Madison in 1845 as "the most cultured and aristocratic town on the stage route from Charleston to New Orleans." Sherman chose not to burn the town, perhaps because one of the people pleading for the town's survival was Senator Joshua Hill, a former college roommate of Sherman's. It's good to have connections.

291. The nation's oldest state park is Indian Springs State Park, formed from lands ceded to the government by the treaty of 1825.

292. Glennville has the world's largest cricket farm.

293. The bones of an ancient whale discovered near Waynesboro may signify a whole new genus. The Vogtle Whale, estimated at 40 million years old, may be the missing link between whales as meat-eating land rovers and the peaceful underseas mammal we know today.

294. The Ladies Garden Club of Athens was America's first garden club.

295. A mile from Lumpkin is a complete village from the 1850s. It covers 58 acres and includes 30 historic buildings moved here from sites all over the state. Daily demonstrations of pioneer baking, spinning, candlemaking, basketweaving and blacksmithing are given. All tools and accouterments are authentic 19th-century pieces from frontier life.

296. Have you hugged a buzzard today? Reed Bingham Park, west of Adel, has an annual Buzzard Day. The park is a major roosting place for black and turkey buzzards, with a thousand or more perches along the three miles of Little River that run through the park.

297. Atlanta is ranked number 2 behind New York City as a computer city. Computer job growth is expected to be high over the next few years.

298. The Macon City Auditorium has the world's largest copper dome. It was built in 1925.

299. Margaret Mitchell, the author of *Gone With The Wind*, was born in Atlanta in 1900. In 1937, she won the Pulitzer prize for her novel.

300. Of the 1,130 species of wildlife in Georgia, 90% are classified as "non-game."

 # GORGEOUS GEORGIA 

301. In Athens at the corner of Dearing and Finley Streets you'll find a tree that owns itself. The land surrounding the tree was deeded to the tree itself by the former owner. In 1942, the original cherished tree was destroyed in a storm, but it was reseeded by its own acorn.

302. The University of Georgia was established in Athens in 1785. It took sixteen years to build the buildings for the first class, a group of ten young men who graduated in 1804.

303. It must be something in the water. Eatonton is the birthplace of Joel Chandler Harris, author and creator of the beloved "Uncle Remus" tales; more recently, native Alice Walker won the Pulitzer Prize for her novel, *The Color Purple.*

304. The Jimmy Carter Library & Museum in Atlanta, houses 27 million pages of documents.

305. Atlanta's Cyclorama, a top tourist destination in Georgia, was created in 1886 by fifteen artists painting on Belgian linen. The nine-ton painting in the round is one of only 20 such panoramas surviving today. It was recently restored at a cost of $11 million by Gustav Berger, who has also restored works by Chagall and Picasso.

306. In Athens, The Moon Lodge meets every full and new moon, combining the worship practices of Celtic, some African, and some Native American origins.

307. Charles Lindbergh got his first plane in Americus and made his first solo flight here in 1923, four years before crossing the Atlantic. He paid $500 for a single-engine Jenny that was sold as World War I military surplus at the aviation training camp in Americus.

308. The only Confederate Naval Museum in the country is in Columbus, which is 252 very dry miles from Savannah and the ocean.

309. The county courthouse in Jonesboro is where Margaret Mitchell spent hours poring over records, looking for names, places and events that would eventually take shape as the epic Civil War saga *Gone With the Wind*.

310. When Alonzo F. Hearndon was born, he was a penniless slave. When he died in Atlanta in 1927, he was a millionaire and the richest black man in the United States.

311. Columbus is known as the "mother-in-law to the army" because so many enlisted men marry local women. Fort Benning, right outside town, is home to the world's largest and most modern infantry training center.

312. The Memory Hill Cemetery in Milledgeville has "slavery-time" graves marked with chains. One chain link dangling over the head of the grave indicates the deceased was born a slave. Two links means he or she was born and lived a slave, and three links means the person buried there was born, lived and died in slavery.

313. In 1989 Columbus became the first city in America to receive the Award of Merit of the International Food, Wine and Travel Writers Association.

314. Hunting is the #1 attraction luring sportsmen from all over the world to South Georgia. Albany has more quail-hunting plantations for paying guests than any where else in the country.

315. Hungry? Stop by the Atlanta State Farmers Market. It spreads over 146 acres and is one of the largest in the world.

316. A Native American chief named the island on Georgia's coast "Cumberland" because the 13-year-old Duke by the same name was kind to the chief's son when they visited England. The Duke gave the boy a gold watch and other favors.

317. Southern author, Flannery O'Connor, is a native of Milledgeville, which was Georgia's first state capital. Augusta and Louisville also served as state capitals before Atlanta was finally chosen.

318. Before the little town of Helen was re-made into a Bavarian Alps village look-alike, it had a scant 300 residents. Now it has three million visitors annually. Its Oktoberfest attracts 300,000 folks. Other festivals include the Alstadt Christmas Market, the Fashing Karnival (a Germanic version of Mardi Gras), Volksmarch, Mayfest, the Annual Hot Air Balloon Race, the Square Dance Festival and an All-American Fourth of July celebration.

319. Fernbank Forest is the last remaining virgin stand of trees in the Appalachian Piedmont region. Some say it may be the last unscathed area of primeval forest in the Southeast. What makes it amazing is that it's right in the middle of Atlanta—65 pristine acres on the northeastern side of the city.

320. Americus may have been named in honor of Americus Vespucius. On the other hand, locals say it may have been named in honor of the "merry cusses" who founded the town. The first place of business was a saloon.

321. The Battle of Bloody Marsh on St. Simons Island in 1742 was the last straw for the Spanish. Shortly after that, they relinquished their hold on North America. Because of that, this battle became one of the most decisive battles in the history of the world.

322. Georgia's annual barbecue cook-off is held the second week of October in Vienna. It's officially named "the Big Pig Jig" but it's also known as the "Redneck Mardi Gras."

323. One of the last battles of the Civil War took place in Columbus in April, 1865.

324. The old White County Courthouse in Cleveland was built with slave labor around 1857 and paid for in Confederate dollars. It's a smaller version of Philadelphia's Independence Hall.

325. In Helen, Georgia, a recreation of a Bavarian Alps village tucked away in the mountains, you can see Charlemagne's Kingdom. It's an elaborate exhibit featuring a miniature Germany, from the North Sea to the Alps, recreating the topographical landscape, bridges, autobahn, towns, villages, lakes, rivers, trains and more.

326. General Lafayette visited Georgia in 1825 and the rolling hills reminded him of home, an estate in France named Chateau de La Grange. LaGrange is named after his estate.

327. Calloway Gardens has the largest glass-enclosed butterfly conservatory in the United States. All 7,000 square feet are designed for nurturing tropical butterflies.

328. When Jimmy Carter became the 39th president, the little town of Plains had 679 people. Seven businesses lined its Main Street, three of which were owned by Carters.

329. Franklin Delano Roosevelt tasted his first moonshine at Warm Springs.

330. Tybee Island, off of Savannah, was settled before Jamestown or Plymouth Rock.

331. Wander into the center of town in Cornelia and feast your eyes on this: A 5,200 pound monument dedicated to apple growers, shaped like a gigantic apple. It's the world's largest apple monument.

332. John D. Rockefeller is said to have refused to join Jekyll Island Club because he thought it was too expensive.

333. At Anna Ruby Falls, take the scenic 4-mile interpretive trail that leads to twin waterfalls. There's also a .15 mile Lion's Eye Trail for visually and physically challenged persons.

334. The foxhunting season in Georgia runs from December until mid-February. Tally-ho!

335. Country music singer Trisha Yearwood lives in Monticello.

336. At the Cotton Exchange in Augusta recently, workers removed several layers of sheetrock and discovered a 45-foot long chalkboard still marked with turn-of-the-century cotton rates.

337. At the thousand-year-old Rock Eagle Effigy Mound, thousands of rocks have been carefully piled into the shape of a huge eagle. It measures 102 feet from wingtip to wingtip. A Creek chief left this warning: "Tread Softly Here White Man, For Long Ere You Came, Strange Races Lived, Fought And Loved."

338. The area known as the Copper Basin at the Georgia-Tennessee border is the result of copper mining in the 1800s. Old mining techniques generated so many toxic copper sulfide fumes that all vegetation in the area was devastated. It has now been reclaimed, but patches of copper-red soil remain to remind us of the area's history.

339. At Fort Yargo State Park, the Will-A-Way Recreation Area was designed for visitors with disabilities, the first of its kind in any state park when it opened in 1971. It's barrier-free, including a fishing bridge. Barrier-free architecture is not what early settlers had in mind. In 1792, they built a blockhouse to protect themselves against native Creek and Cherokee.

340. Eli Whitney put the finishing touches on his cotton gin while staying at Cumberland Island's manor house, Dungeness.

341. Georgia has 275 airports and 89 heliports.

342. "Turn left at the big chicken." No, it's not a joke. It's a 56-foot tall sheet-metal rooster that rules over the road on the corner of Highway 41 and Roswell Road near Marietta. It's so big, pilots use it for a reference point.

343. Underground Atlanta used to be the train station for Western & Atlantic Railroads in the 1800s, and became the hub of the business area. Now it's a six block complex of restaurants, shops and cabarets. You can walk through Atlanta's colorful history at the 7,000 square foot Heritage Row on upper Alabama Strcct, a projcct that cost $2.7 million.

344. Bob's Candies was founded by Bob McCormick in Albany. His uncle, Catholic priest Gregory Keller, invented a machine that stretched, twisted, cut and bent candy canes automatically.

345. The Appalachian Trail is the oldest, continuously marked footpath in the world. At the Walasa-Yi Center is a stone arch, the only place the trail passes under a structure made with human hands. The Georgia portion of the trail is considered to be the most rugged.

346. No one knows if any of Blackbeard's loot is buried on the 5,618 acre island that bears his name. Blackbeard himself said "Nobody but the devil and myself know where my treasure is, and the longer liver of the two shall have it all." The island is preserved as natural refuge, but swimming and shelling is permitted. How long is your liver?

347. Atlanta is the headquarters of the Turner Broadcasting System, a major cable-television company that in 1980 established the Cable News Network. In 1982, CNN originated the first live American telecast from Cuba since 1958. In August 1991, CNN was first with news and live coverage of the coup d'etat in the Soviet Union. It is now the largest and most profitable news and information company in the world.

348. Savannah has the first Moravian church established in the New World, built in 1736.

349. The remains of the Spanish Conquistador's northernmost mission can be found on St. Catherines Island.

350. Hughston Clinic, Columbus's Institute of Sports Medicine, was the first of its kind in the world.

351. A piece of armor unearthed at DeSoto Falls gave the park its name. It's believed that the armor belonged to someone in the legendary explorer's party when he passed through Georgia in 1540.

352. The largest black educational complex in the world is in Atlanta.

353. Glennville farmers grow certified Vidalia onions, and boast their very own onion festival, just like Vidalia, down the road.

354. Jimmy Carter got his start in politics by representing Americus and Sumter County in the state legislature.

355. At the Fred Hamilton Rhododendron Gardens in Towns County, there are over 2,000 rhododendrons, azaleas and wildflowers. They're in bloom sometime between mid-April to June.

356. In 1828, a hunter named Benjamin Parks kicked up a lump of something that he said looked like "the yellow of an egg." It was gold, and Parks sparked the nation's first gold rush in Georgia's mountains.

357. General Sherman considered Savannah too beautiful to burn. He gave it to Abraham Lincoln as a Christmas gift. "I beg to present you, as a Christmas gift, the City of Savannah," he telegraphed the President in 1864.

358. In Albany is the state's largest natural spring, Radium Springs. You won't glow in the dark if you swim there. Really.

359. Techwood, near Georgia Tech in Atlanta, was the nation's first federal public housing project. It was dedicated by President Roosevelt in 1936.

360. The Georgia motto is "Wisdom, Justice, and Moderation." The state song is "Georgia on My Mind," words by Stuart Gorell and music by Hoagy Carmichael.

361. Traditional Appalachian farmers believed in astrology. They based their decisions about planting and harvesting on the zodiac and the phases of the moon, and even consult the night sky before getting a haircut or painting the barn.

362. Savannah is in the top ten US cities for walking tours. You can take a tour catering to your love of historic houses, architecture, ghosts, civil war history, gardens or many other whims.

363. Martin Luther King was born in Atlanta in 1929, and was buried there in 1968. His home is part of the Sweet Auburn historic district.

364. I-75 to Florida is one of the busiest stretches of freeway in the country.

365. Stone Mountain, a massive outcropping of granite near Atlanta, has a climate more like a desert than the lush semi-tropical environment typical to the South. The rock holds little soil, retains the heat and retains very little water. As a result, it supports a unique geology, botany and animal life. One rare plant found clinging to its surface is the Confederate Yellow Daisy.

366. It may be the real thing, but no one really knows where it started. Atlanta natives say Coca-Cola was first created in a brass kettle on Marietta Street in their home town. Visit Columbus, and you'll hear that Dr. John Pemberton cooked it up there. Dr. Pemberton was a Confederate general who touted the beverage as "the French wine of Coca." He sold the formula for either $283.14 or $1750, and died penniless in 1888.

367. The first nuclear-powered merchant ship was named the NS Savannah and sailed from the port of Savannah in 1912.

368. The town of Decatur was founded in 1823. Worried about noise and pollution, the city fathers refused to let the railroad stop in their town. The next community, Terminus, was chosen as a major stop instead. It grew into the city we now call Atlanta.

369. The R.J. Reynolds mansion on Sapelo Island was the first air conditioned home in the South. Charles Lindbergh, Calvin Coolidge and others were guests here.

370. Eddie Owens Martin, who called himself "St. EOM," was born in 1908. The eccentric visionary built Pasaquan, a bizarre garden of molded, sculpted and painted concrete and wood found near Columbus. Martin died in 1986.

371. Sapelo Island has been called the most homogeneous, direct link to Black Africa in the Western Hemisphere.

372. At The World of Coca-Cola in Atlanta, a huge exhibit touting the commercial success of this Southern creation, the price of admission includes all the Coca-Cola you can drink. Have a Coke and a smile.

373. Cuthbert is famous for its turkey-calling contest. They don't use telephones.This little town is also known as the birthplace of jazz great Fletcher H. Henderson Jr.

374. The largest public lakeside beach in Georgia is at John Tanner State Park.

375. In 1990, approximately 63 percent of all Georgians lived in areas defined as urban, and the rest in rural areas.

376. The Southern Christian Leadership Conference was founded by Martin Luther King Jr. in the basement of the Ebenezer Baptist Church in Atlanta in 1957.

377. A 19th century municipal ordinance in Savannah made it illegal for "ugly, maimed or diseased" individuals to use city streets.

378. Musician James Brown lives in Augusta and started his career in Macon.

379. De Soto heard about giants who lived in the Okefenokee Swamp and never ventured in. Skeletal remains verify a race of Native Americans living there who were uncommonly large.

380. The Arts Festival of Atlanta is one of the oldest and largest in the country. It's held every September.

381. Don't bother bringing your surfboard. The average wave size off the Georgia coast is one foot—lower than any other on the Eastern seaboard.

382. Atlantans spend more per capita eating out than natives of Washington, D.C., Los Angeles, Houston or San Diego.

GORGEOUS GEORGIA

383. Lake Seminole is ranked among the top five bass fishing spots in the country. Large mouth and white bass are found in the relatively shallow lake, in addition to stripers, bream and crappie. There are more fish varieties in this lake than in any other lake in the state.

384. Colquitt is the Mayhaw Capital of the World. Mayhaws are called berries, but they're technically related to the apple. They have a faint guava taste.

385. It's a Southern thing. The Cherokees who first lived in Georgia took their ball games very seriously, just like current residents. The outcome of a game was frequently a life-or-death issue.

386. There's only one so-called "Native American mansion" in all of the country, but that may be a dubious distinction. Chief Vann's house is in Chatsworth, and it's open to the public.

387. The formal gardens at Merchants Hope Village have the only hemlock maze in America grown in the traditional British style.

388. If Sherman had ridden a bike, would he have been a little less sore at the Rebels? There's no way to know, but you can retrace Sherman's path on a bicycle "March to the Sea." It's a 475-mile trek starting in Rossville and ending in fair Savannah.

389. Between all his other activities, Benito Mussolini found time to give the city of Rome, Georgia a reproduction of the famous statue of the she-wolf suckling the orphans Romulus and Remus. It's said that the two brothers disagreed about whose name would adorn the ancient city now known as Rome, and Romulus won the argument by killing his brother. The reproduction is now in front of City Hall in Rome, Georgia.

390. Early visitors to the Southern Appalachians compared the area to the Garden of Eden, with ample reason. There are more than 1500 types of blooming plants, and 130 varieties of trees, compared to only 85 tree varieties in all of Europe.

391. In retrospect, some decisions are hazardous to your health. On behalf of the Cherokees, Major Ridge signed a treaty with government authorities which led to the Cherokee removal and the infamous Trail of Tears. When he followed his fellow tribesmen to Oklahoma, he was executed for selling off tribal lands. His house in Georgia, the Chieftain's Museum, was first a cabin built in 1794 and later expanded.

392. The first silk exported from this continent left from the port of Savannah. Silk never really took off as a product of Georgia, although several different entrepreneurs gave it a spin.

GORGEOUS GEORGIA

393. The *New York Times* called Atlanta's High Museum "among the best any city has built in at least a generation."

394. Metropolitan Atlanta has 36 colleges and universities within its borders.

395. Mountains in North Georgia are sometimes topped with bare patches called "balds." There's no explanation for the phenomenon—the mountains aren't high enough for trees to stop growing because of altitude. Some speculate that forest growth stops abruptly because of scars left by long-past fires, or perhaps these balds are ancient Native American sacred grounds.

396. Mrs. Wilke's Boarding House in Savannah is ranked among the country's top fifteen restaurants. You can go to the back door for take out orders.

397. Blue Ridge settlers learned quickly about the value of the man-shaped ginseng root that grows wild in the hills. As early as the 18th century, "'sang" hunters gathered the herb for sale to China, where it was believed to have great restorative powers. Ginseng is also found in many Appalachian folk remedies. It is more potent when found in the wild.

398. Swine Time is celebrated in Climax the Saturday after Thanksgiving. Camilla holds an annual Gnat Days festival the second and third weekends in June.

399. *Conde Nast Traveler* calls Savannah "one of the top ten U.S. cities to visit," and *LeMonde* calls it "the most beautiful city in North America."

400. Savannah is the hometown of Supreme Court Justice Clarence Thomas.

401. St. Mary's River, which divides Florida from Georgia, is one of the crookedest rivers in the world.

402. The Allman Brothers Band is from Georgia; Duane Allman died in a tragic motorcycle accident in Macon in 1971.

403. According to folks who know, War Woman Dell is one of the most powerful spots in Georgia for recharging your psychic energy.

404. Woodrow Wilson married his first wife, Ellen Axson of Rome, in 1885. They had three daughters. Mrs. Wilson was such a sweet woman that when Congress heard she was ill and likely to die, they hurried to pass a bill for slum clearance in Washington, knowing it was a subject near to her heart. They passed it in time for her to hear of it before her death, in August, 1914.

405. No matter where you are, you're likely to see lots of trees. About 60 percent of Georgia's land area is covered with forest. Slash and longleaf pine mingle with hardwood trees like the large live oak in the coastal woodlands. Low-lying areas feature marsh grasses and swamp trees like cypress and tupelo. The forest in the Piedmont region is mainly a mixture of oak and pine. In northern Georgia the forest covering the mountains is composed principally of oak, hickory, maple, and other hardwood trees. Flowering trees and shrubs like redbud, dogwood, and azalea are found throughout the state, even in urban areas.

406. William McKinley made his decision to run for president of the United States while visiting Thomasville in the 1890s. He was a native of Ohio, and was elected president twice, although he was assassinated before completing his second term.

407. The Blue Ridge is the rainiest part of state, because moist marine air is forced to rise when it meets the mountains.

408. In the 1990 census, the state's biggest cities were Atlanta, the capital; Columbus; Savannah; Macon; and Albany.

409. Some turtles share dens with alligators in the Okefenokee Swamp. The compact nature of the swamp means a dense population of wildlife. It also means that those turtles are pretty mean.

410. According to the 1990 census, Georgia had 6,478,216 inhabitants, an increase of 18.6 percent over 1980.

411. About 40,000 runners annually participate in the Peachtree Road Race every year in Atlanta.

412. Elevations range from sea level, along the Atlantic Ocean, to 4784 feet, atop Brasstown Bald, near the northern boundary.

413. After the Civil War, Georgia was not restored to the Union until July, 1870.

414. Calloway Gardens has the largest manmade inland beach in the world. But you have to pay to get in.

415. Many U.S. Presidents have found Georgia's charms irresistible: Franklin D. Roosevelt, George Washington, William Taft, Calvin Coolidge and William McKinley, to name a few.

416. Georgia is named for George II of England and is known as the Empire State of the South.

417. Atlanta is ranked in the top four cities for the most Fortune 500 corporate headquarters.

418. After Union troops captured Fort Pulaski, they didn't expend a whole lot of effort for the rest of the war, according to their neighbors in Savannah. Some folks even say they spent their time playing baseball. Now, locals host period-costumed ball games at the fort in honor of these languid Yankees.

419. In 1989, Rand McNally's *Retirement Places Rated Guide* said Clayton and Clarkesville in Northeast Georgia were second only to Lake Murray in Kentucky. as a great place to spend your golden years. On April 9th, 1997, *The Wall Street Journal* also gave a nod to Clarkesville calling it the best place to live in Georgia.

420. The Blue Ridge Mountains, with their Southern terminus in Northeast Georgia, are the oldest mountains on the North American continent and may be the oldest mountains in the world.

421. The Okefenokee is one of the most noteworthy examples of an ecologically intact swamp in North America. Native Americans first inhabited the area 4,000 years ago. It's a huge, ancient peat bog that used to be part of the ocean floor. Now, it ranges in elevation from 103 to 128 feet above sea level.

422. The New York Zoological Society operates a captive breeding program for endangered species on St. Catherines Island.

423. James Lord Pierpont was living in Savannah in 1857 when he composed "Jingle Bells." He served with the First Georgia Calvary during the Civil War and wrote Confederate music.

424. "Savannah Gray" bricks, used to build many historic homes and other structures, take their distinctive color from the local sandy soil.

425. We should all be so lucky...after heavy rains the employees of water treatment plants in Atlanta have found gold nuggets. Although America's first gold rush ended in 1849, runoff from rivers like the Chattahoochee and Peachtree Creek still contains small amounts of the metal.

426. The Savannah Theatre is the oldest continuously operating theatre site in the country.

427. Off the Georgia coast, you can take a kayak trip and hike into one of the last stands of virgin Tidewater Cypress trees. Some are more than 1300 years old.

428. Georgia is one of the top film locations in the country. Last year, $92.5 million was spent on making feature films and television movies.

429. You can go to the Athens Commerce Drive-in for first- and second-run movies. It's one of about 500 drive-in theatres left in the world. At the peak of their popularity in 1958, there were 4,063 drive-ins in the country.

430. *Money Magazine* named Albany to its "Top City List" in 1997. Albany ranked 112th in the nation based on economics, health, crime, housing, education, weather, transit, leisure and the arts.

431. Wine production in Georgia began in the 1730s, but viniculture has only enjoyed a renaissance in the last decade. There are currently six wineries in the state.

432. SciTrek, in Atlanta, is ranked among the top ten science centers in the nation. It opened in October 1988, and houses over 150 permanent interactive exhibits. It is nonprofit and privately funded.

433. When General James Oglethorpe settled Georgia in 1733, he envisioned a utopian community where alcohol, slavery and speculation were outlawed, and where religious persecution and oppressive class differences would be abolished. Nice try, General!

434. Georgia ranks 14th in the number of pleasure boats it operates—298,000.

435. Georgia hosted one million anglers in 1996, who fished a total of 14.9 million days. All together, they spent $1.2 billion on fishing, including travel costs, food and lodging, and equipment. Plus the cost of worms, of course.

436. Alice Coachman Davis was the first black woman to win an Olympic Gold Medal. A medalist in the high jump competition in 1948, she was born in Albany in 1922. There's a park named in her honor in her hometown.

437. The annual commercial seafood landing is about 11,268,000 pounds and has a total value of approximately $21,573,000. Edible shellfish make up the bulk of the catch in terms of both volume and value, and shrimp is the leading variety landed. Crabs, oysters, and clams are caught also.

438. Cumberland is the largest and southernmost barrier island in Georgia's chain of sea islands, separated from the mainland by salt marsh, rivers and sound. Cumberland's vast pristine beaches, interior live oak forests, abundant wildlife and famous wild horses are all national natural treasures.

439. Watch your step in the Okefenokee Swamp. The "land" there is formed by layers of peat covered by grasses, shrubs and trees. When stepped on, the ground moves a bit, which is why the Indians called the swamp "trembling earth," or "Okefenokee".

440. Sherman stopped here: Fort McAllister was the end of Sherman's march to the sea, and now is one of the most beautiful state parks on Georgia's coast. The earthen underground forts built by Confederate soldiers are some of the best preserved in the country.

441. When Duane Allman was asked what he was doing about the war in Vietnam, he replied that every time he went home to Georgia he ate a peach for peace. The Allman Brothers Band produced an album titled "Eat A Peach" in 1972.

Notes

Notes

Premium gift books from PREMIUM PRESS AMERICA include:

TITANIC TRIVIA

BILL DANCES TREASURY OF
FISHING TIPS
(available spring 1998)

GREAT AMERICAN COUNTRY
MUSIC

GREAT AMERICAN STOCK CAR
RACING

GREAT AMERICAN WOMEN
(available summer 1998)

GREAT AMERICAN GOLF
(available summer of 1998)

GREAT AMERICAN CIVIL WAR
(available summer 1998)

I'LL BE DOGGONE
CATS OUT OF THE BAG

STOCK CAR TRIVIA ENCYCLOPEDIA
STOCK CAR FUN & GAMES
STOCK CAR DRIVERS & TRACKS
STOCK CAR LEGENDS

AMAZING ARKANSAS
ABSOLUTELY ALABAMA
FABULOUS FLORIDA
(available summer 1998)
GORGEOUS GEORGIA
TERRIFIC TENNESSEE
VINTAGE VIRGINIA

To order or for more information contact:

PREMIUM PRESS AMERICA
P.O. Box 159015
Nashville, Tn 37215-9015
(800) 891-7323
(615) 256-8484 office
(615) 256-8624 fax

PREMIUM PRESS AMERICA books are available in bookstores and gift shops everywhere. If, by chance, none are carried in your local area books can be ordered direct from the Publisher. All premium books are $6.95 plus $2.00 for shipping & handling. Quantity discounts are available. Expect delivery in 7-10 days.